# The Daylight Limited

BY **LIN OLIVER**    ILLUSTRATED BY **CHARLES S. PYLE**

*GREAT RAILWAY ADVENTURES*
*SERIES 1 • ADVENTURE 1*
*Learning Curve Publishing*
*Chicago*

For Theo, Oliver, and Cole . . .
my Biggleton, Middleton, and Littleton — L.O.

To my dad, who escaped to San Francisco on
the Coast Daylight — C.P.

THE GREAT RAILWAY ADVENTURES BOOKS ARE IN MEMORY OF
MURRAY SCHRAMM, GREAT FRIEND AND MENTOR.

Library of Congress Catalog Card Number: 98-85455

ISBN 1-890647-50-0 (hardbound)
ISBN 1-890647-53-5 (paperback)

10 9 8 7 6 5 4 3

Special thanks to Taylor Bruce and Craig Marshall, the train crew who artfully
added color to this story. — C.P.

Text set in 14 point Simoncini Garamond
Art direction and text design by Joy Chu

Printed in Hong Kong

*It was well known in*

the town of San Luis Obispo that the Holden family loved trains.
Every afternoon, when they heard the train whistle, they would stop their chores to
watch the *Daylight Limited* thunder along the tracks.

Mr. and Mrs. Holden would wave at the engineer. Tuck and Billie would chase the
sleek orange engine until they fell down, exhausted. Chief wagged his tail so hard that
it looked like his backside was going to fall off.

"There's something about a train that makes a person feel alive," Mr. Holden
would say.

One night, Tuck had a dream that he was riding in a train car made of glass.

"I saw mountains and sky all around me," he told his family. "It was like being in a huge moving window."

Mr. Holden always listened carefully to his children.

"I think you've got an idea there, son," he said.

Mrs. Holden, who had an artistic flair, drew a picture of Tuck's dream train car. It had a great domed roof made of glass and comfortable chairs where a person could watch the world whiz by.

Mr. Holden, who loved to tinker in his workshop, studied his wife's picture.

"I'm going to build that," he said.

Mr. Holden spent many days and nights constructing a perfect model. Tuck helped, asking questions and offering ideas.

"Let's call it the Tucker," he suggested.

"That's not fair," said Billie. "I want a train car named after me, too."

"How about the Chief?" said Tuck. Chief wagged his tail heartily.

"Too late," said Mr. Holden. "There already is a train called the *Chief*."

"I think we should call it the Dome Car," Mrs. Holden said simply. She had a way of getting to the heart of the matter.

When the model of the Dome Car was finished, it was like a real train car in every way. The wheels turned and the doors opened. The windows arched up to the sky, and inside were chairs that swiveled. There was even a cord that the crew could pull to sound whistle signals — two short blasts to go forward, four short blasts to brake.

Tuck and his father proudly showed their invention to the engineer of the *Daylight Limited.*

"A train made of glass!" The engineer chuckled. He held his sides and laughed so hard he popped a button off his overalls.

Mrs. Fernandez, who worked at the ticket window, didn't laugh. Instead, she showed Tuck and Mr. Holden a poster on the station wall. It said:

*VISIT THE INVENTION OF TOMORROW CONTEST JUNE 26, 1939, AT THE NEW YORK WORLD'S FAIR!*

"You should take your invention to the World's Fair," she suggested. "It's the place for big ideas."

"The Invention of Tomorrow," said Tuck, his eyes shining with excitement. "That's perfect. We'll win the contest and then everyone will know about our Dome Car. We'll be famous."

"Tuck, you must be dreaming," Mr. Holden said.

"This is America." Mrs. Fernandez smiled. "Everyone is entitled to dream."

The Holdens took a vote. It was five to zero in favor of entering the contest.

"This is fine and dandy," pointed out Mr. Holden, "but New York is all the way across the country. How will we pay for the tickets?"

"I'll sell my comic books and catcher's mitt," said Tuck.

"I'll sell my gold locket," said Billie.

"I have a few dollars I've been saving for a rainy day," said Mrs. Holden.

There was still only enough money to buy two tickets. It was agreed that Tuck, Billie, and Chief would stay behind with Cousin Ida. Mr. and Mrs. Holden would ride the *Daylight Limited* to San Francisco, where they would pick up the overland route to New York.

At the station, the family stood silently waiting for the train. From a distance, they heard four short blasts of the whistle. They all knew what that meant. The *Daylight Limited* was putting on the brakes and coming into town.

Mr. Holden took Tuck and Billie in his arms. "I want you both to remember something," he said. "No matter how far away your mother and I are, we'll always be just on the other side of that whistle."

Mr. Holden gave his children a long hug. Mrs. Holden blew kisses. Billie and Tuck did not stop waving until the train was out of sight.

Cousin Ida arrived that day. She wore sensible shoes and had a rule for everything. She made brussels sprouts for dinner and put starch in the sheets. She insisted on baths and would not allow whispering after the lights were out. Cousin Ida had no use for fun. When Chief brought her his rubber ball to toss, she locked it in a drawer and said, "Who does he think I am, Babe Ruth?"

Tuck checked off each day on the calendar. The Invention of Tomorrow contest was five days away.

"If only we could be there." Billie sighed.

Outside, Tuck and Billie could hear the *Daylight Limited* approaching. The sound of the whistle made them think of their mother and father. They knew that somewhere on their way to New York City, their parents were thinking of them, too.

The next day, Cousin Ida went to the train station to pick up a package.

"You children are to wait for me on the platform," she said. "No wandering away. No unnecessary giggling. No teasing or wrestling. No buying of candy or kicking of cans."

Cousin Ida turned to Chief. "As for you," she said, "no barking, no biting, no scratching, no whimpering — no anything."

Satisfied that the rules had been laid down, Cousin Ida disappeared into the depot. The *Daylight Limited* was stopped in the station, sitting on the tracks like a snake sleeping in the sun.

The smell of food floated from the dining car. Chief sniffed. There was steak in the air. Chief loved steak. He jumped from the bench, bounded across the platform, and leaped onto the train. Tuck and Billie ran after him.

Chief dashed through the dining car, following his nose to the kitchen.

"Who do we have here?" The chef smiled.

"I'm sorry, mister," Billie said breathlessly. "Our dog smelled food."

"He must be hungry," said the chef. "I was just whipping up a little dinner for Gypsy, Miss LaRue's dog. There's some left over."

"Loretta LaRue is on this train?" asked Tuck, his eyes opening wide. She was the most famous movie star in Hollywood. "Could I get her autograph?"

"Miss LaRue has a private car all the way at the end of the train," said the chef. "She doesn't like visitors."

"But she's Tuck's all-time favorite star," said Billie. "It would mean so much to him."

The chef scratched his chin. "I'll make you a deal," he said to Tuck. "If you promise not to be a pest, I'll let you deliver Gypsy's dinner. At least you'll get to see Miss LaRue."

Tuck grinned and shook the chef's hand so hard that he finally had to ask Tuck to stop.

With Gypsy's dinner in hand, Tuck and Billie were heading to Loretta LaRue's private car when the engine suddenly shot out a cloud of white steam.

"All aboo-ard," the conductor called. "Next stop . . . San Francisco."

"Billie, the train is leaving!" exclaimed Tuck.

Another blast of steam rose up. The train lurched forward. "Uh-oh," said Billie. "We're moving!"

Billie grabbed Chief, and they tried to get to the exit, pushing their way through the crowded parlor car.

The train picked up speed. The clickity-clack of the wheels grew louder and faster. Tuck looked out the window. The station was far back in the distance now. Up ahead, he could see the pine-covered mountains that ran along the California coast.

"Looks like we're going to San Francisco," Tuck said.

Billie giggled. This was definitely against Cousin Ida's rules.

Loretta LaRue's name was written in gold letters on the door of her private car. Tuck knocked. Billie and Chief waited in the shadows.

"Who is it?" came the throaty voice from inside.

"I've brought Gypsy's dinner," said Tuck.

The door flew open and there stood Loretta LaRue.

"Thank goodness, you're here," she said. "Gypsy was getting very cranky. Come in."

Loretta sat down on a red velvet chair.

"Put the bowl near me," she said to Tuck. "Gypsy doesn't like to eat alone."

Loretta looked out the window as the *Daylight Limited* chugged up the mountain pass.
Large rocks were scattered on top of jagged cliffs.

"This view reminds me of when I made *Rio Rojo*," she said. "Did you see that movie?"

"Three times, ma'am," answered Tuck.

"You're a good boy." She smiled.

Suddenly, Tuck heard a rumbling noise. He looked out the window and what he saw made his heart pound fast. Several of the rocks had come loose and were tumbling down the mountain, heading right toward them.

"Watch out!" Tuck yelled. "It's a rock slide!"

*Smack!* Rocks pounded into their car. *Crash!* A large rock hit the train just where Loretta's car connected to the one in front.

"Oh, no!" Tuck moaned. "The coupler has been hit!"

"What's a coupler?" screamed Loretta.

"It's what hooks us up to the rest of the train," said Tuck. "Ours is broken almost in half!"

"What will become of us?" cried Loretta.

Tuck looked at the twisted metal coupler. He had a sinking feeling in the bottom of his stomach.

The coupler held for a moment, but it was too damaged to last. It rattled and shook under the strain.

"Help!" sobbed Loretta. "We're coming undone."

The weakened hook gave way. Loretta's car broke away from the *Daylight Limited* and began to slide back, picking up speed as it rolled down the steep grade.

Billie stared in horror.

"My brother's in there!" she screamed. "We have to stop that car."

"They have a hand brake inside," said the conductor, "but Miss LaRue doesn't even know it's there."

"I'll tell Tuck," said Billie.

"They're halfway down the mountain," said the conductor. "He can't hear you."

"Yes, he can," said Billie. "Just get me to the whistle."

Billie and Chief ran after the conductor. There was no time to lose.

Billie knew that Tuck would understand her. Their father had taught them all about whistle signals: Two short blasts to go forward. Four short blasts to brake.

She took hold of the whistle cord and pulled.

The car with Tuck and Loretta inside was zooming downhill faster than a roller coaster. Tuck felt as if they were going to fly right off the tracks. The accident had happened so fast. He was afraid, very afraid, and he didn't know what to do. Then he heard the whistle.

One . . . two . . . three . . . four — four short blasts! It was the signal to brake!

"Is there a hand brake in here?" Tuck shouted to Loretta.

"I'm an actress," she cried. "I make entrances and exits. I don't know anything about trains."

Tuck looked all over the car but he could not find the brake. Again he heard four short blasts. Billie was talking to him from the engine, telling him to find the brake. It was nowhere to be seen.

Tuck's eyes scanned every detail of the car — the polished oak panels . . . the silk window shades . . . Loretta's pink feathered hat hanging on the wall —

"The hat!" Tuck cried. "It's just what I've been looking for."

"Don't be silly," said Loretta. "Pink is definitely not your color."

Tuck yanked the hat off the wall. *The brake!*

He pulled it as hard as he could.

"I thought that was an odd place for a hat rack," said Loretta.

The mighty brakes screeched.
Sparks flew. Time seemed to stand still.
The speeding car ground to a stop.

When the *Daylight Limited* pulled into the San Francisco station, all the passengers, including Tuck and Loretta, were tired, but safe.

The train officials gathered around Loretta as she described their hair-raising adventure, dabbing at her eyes with a handkerchief.

"This boy is a true hero," she said, taking Tuck's hand. "He saved our lives."

"With a lot of help from my sister," Tuck said.

"How can I ever thank you, children?" Loretta said. "Please tell me what I can do. Anything."

"Anything?" asked Tuck.

"Anything at all," said Loretta.

Tuck and Billie smiled at each other. They were thinking the same thing.

That night, Tuck and Billie and Chief left San Francisco on the train bound for New York City. They were riding in a deluxe compartment, courtesy of Miss Loretta LaRue.

Wouldn't their parents be surprised to see them at the World's Fair! With luck, the Dome Car would win the Invention of Tomorrow contest, and their whole family would be together to see their dream come true.

The train whistle blew as Tuck and Billie crawled into their snug berths. They slept soundly, knowing that their parents were just on the other side of that whistle. It wouldn't be long before they'd all be together again.

# The Daylight Limited

You might not realize that trains have a rich and colorful history. If you enjoyed reading The Daylight Limited, these train facts may interest you.

**DID YOU KNOW THAT . . .**

• The first trains in the early 1800s were pulled by horses, not engines.

• One of the first steam engines in the United States was called the *Tom Thumb*. In 1830 it raced against a horse-drawn train. The steam engine lost!

• Andrew Jackson was the first American president to ride on a train. The year was 1833.

• When trains crossed the western plains in the 1800s, they were often delayed for hours by herds of buffalo crossing the tracks.

• In the early days of train travel, trains had no headlights. To see at night, train crews built a bonfire on a flatcar in front of the engine. The sparks from the fire often started brush fires.

• The ceilings on early train cars were so low that some adults would bump their heads if they stood up straight.

• In 1863, the first dining cars were introduced. In 1865, George Pullman built the first sleeping car called the *Pioneer*. In 1867, hotel cars with dining and sleeping compartments were placed into service. ✍

• At one time, there were more than twenty different track widths, or gauges. Different trains traveled on different size tracks. When the track size changed, passengers had to get off and switch to another train. It wasn't until 1886 that the railroad companies agreed upon a standard track width — 4 feet, 8 ½ inches.

• The longest freight train ever measured in the United States was nearly four miles long. It had 500 coal cars.

If you want to learn more about trains, ask your librarian for suggestions. There are many wonderful books on train travel, the history of trains, and model trains.

❡ *The* Daylight *trains, once billed as the most beautiful in America, began service in 1937 and ran daily from Los Angeles to San Francisco.*